Free The Bird

A poetry collection by Wildwood Writer

Free The Bird by Virginia Helena Guarddon Pueyo (Wildwood
Writer)

Copyright © 2022 by Virginia H. Guarddon Pueyo.

For permission requests, contact:

Wildwood Publishing

Instagram Message: @wildwoodwriter

First Edition: 2024

This book is a collection of poetry. Names, characters, places,
and incidents either are the product of the author's
imagination or are used fictitiously. Any resemblance to
actual events, locales, or persons, living or dead, is
coincidental.

Cover Design and Art Throughout:

by Pexels Photos & IStock photos

Free The Bird

a poetry collection by Virginia Guarddon

In this collection of verses, dive into the raw currents of emotion, vivid images, and personal revelations flowing from the ink's depth. Each poem serves as a bold stroke on the canvas of the soul, inviting you to join a journey marked by healing, beauty, and profound connections.

Feel the embrace of nature as it becomes my silent healer, weaving its magic through the verses. Experience the weight of sadness, the sacrifice of leaving behind all that was familiar, including the separation from my husband during the healing process.

Witness how my husband's presence became the inspiration for these words, a testament to our enduring love, resilient even across the distances. Follow the path of my triumphant rise, the culmination of healing, as I step into the role I've always yearned for - a writer.

Simple and raw, my words spill across the pages, narrating a life's journey. Allow these verses to unfold, revealing a universe ready to be explored, felt, and embraced.

Dedication

To the unwavering love and encouragement of my
muse, my devoted husband, who has breathed life
into my words and kindled the fire within my soul.
To my children, the radiant source of inspiration,
whose belief in my dreams fuels the fight within me
and to my parents, who instilled in me a love for
language and the courage to share it.

Table of Contents

Preface

Within these pages, you'll find the unfiltered
journey of Virginia Guarddon—a life painted in raw
simplicity. Born in the Canary Islands, her story
unfolds across dance stages, piano keys, and the
profound power of words.

In the winter of 2022, a life-altering accident led
her back to the Canary Islands, separating her from
family and prompting the arduous task of rebuilding
connections.

This collection of verses isn't just poetry; it's a
spillage of raw emotion, capturing the subtleties of
human experience and the untouched beauty of
nature.

Dear reader, immerse yourself in these pages where
simplicity meets complexity, where rawness dances
with refinement. In each verse, you may find echoes
of your own journey as we navigate life's tapestry
together, one word at a time.

How beautiful it is to spill

your authenticity over paper

as if your soul was ink

for others to soak in.

Nature Is My Healer

1

Soft sea, sand and stillness,

A bird's song.

This is what I call home.

Wild Sap

I am like the sap

that bleeds from a tree,

earthy and robust,

with a lingering flavor.

The taste of a wooded forest,

with night creatures,

under a starlight sky.

Deep Roots:

And one truth remains;

everything that lives also grows.

I ponder the way trees

Root deeply in the cold earth,

nourishing themselves from the soil,

Feeding trunk, leaves, and flowers,

sipping life from the earth

to stand tall and forceful

Against the sky, the sun, the clouds.

I often wonder

if I can do the same.

I've always wanted to be a tree,

sturdy and strong,

tall and unapologetic.

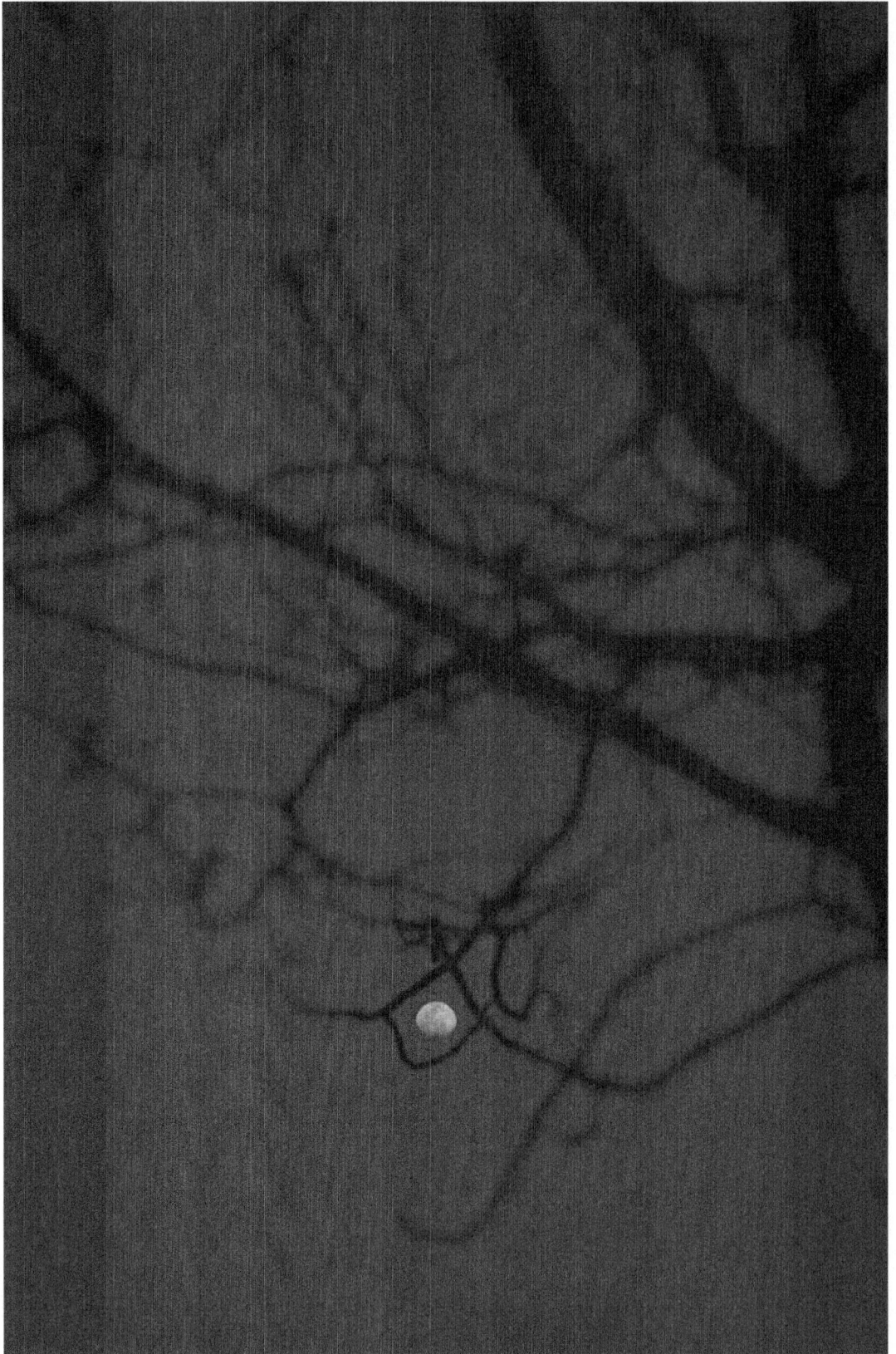

Breath Of Life

The wind, translucent creature of the unseen,

Always makes itself known.

Its presence is felt, softly or mighty,

Its mood dictates the flow.

When in fury—windows fly open, doors loudly shut,

A baby's cry rides its rage, unwelcome.

As calm rises, it quiets the sky,

Tenderly brushing the green fields of grass.

Maybe, its fickle nature is a veiled gift,

Pollen and seeds scattered over Gaia's womb,

The breath of life.

Pale Beams

The moon hangs high in the stark sky,

Swallowing the night with its silver sigh.

My muse, it shares its pale beams,

Competing fiercely 'gainst the starry streams.

It guides me through the darkened sight,

While wolves serenade to its glowing light.

And here I wander, far from the chaos,

Letting the moonrise cleanse me whole.

Silver Moon

I wake in black,

Exploring your darkness

like an owl in flight.

All night, my bat-like eyes

flutter among the woods.

I rise to watch—

A wave of fireflies

arises before my eyes,

And there you are,

Moon, silver as a mirror,

Breaking through the veil of night.

Counting Seconds

I look around,

Counting three seconds,

Eyelids rise, one by one,

A second glance,

Nature explodes in bloom.

Spring crashes in,

Flowers carpet the earth.

I ache to seize this beauty

In a single breath,

Inhaling deeply, as if to cage it within.

Oxygen floods each lung, expanding,

I feel alive.

Nocturnal

I wander through the woods,

in search of myself,

amidst the night creatures.

There is release in the stillness of the night.

Moss blankets the ground,

a green sheet of life against the pitch-black.

Sometimes, this kind of quiet

births small miracles deep in the soul.

Nude Fruit

I wake each day, curious,

wondering what kind of softness

changed me through the years.

I've lost many of my human fragments,

laying like ancient, nude fruit,

ready to be swallowed.

I need to be restored,

become whole.

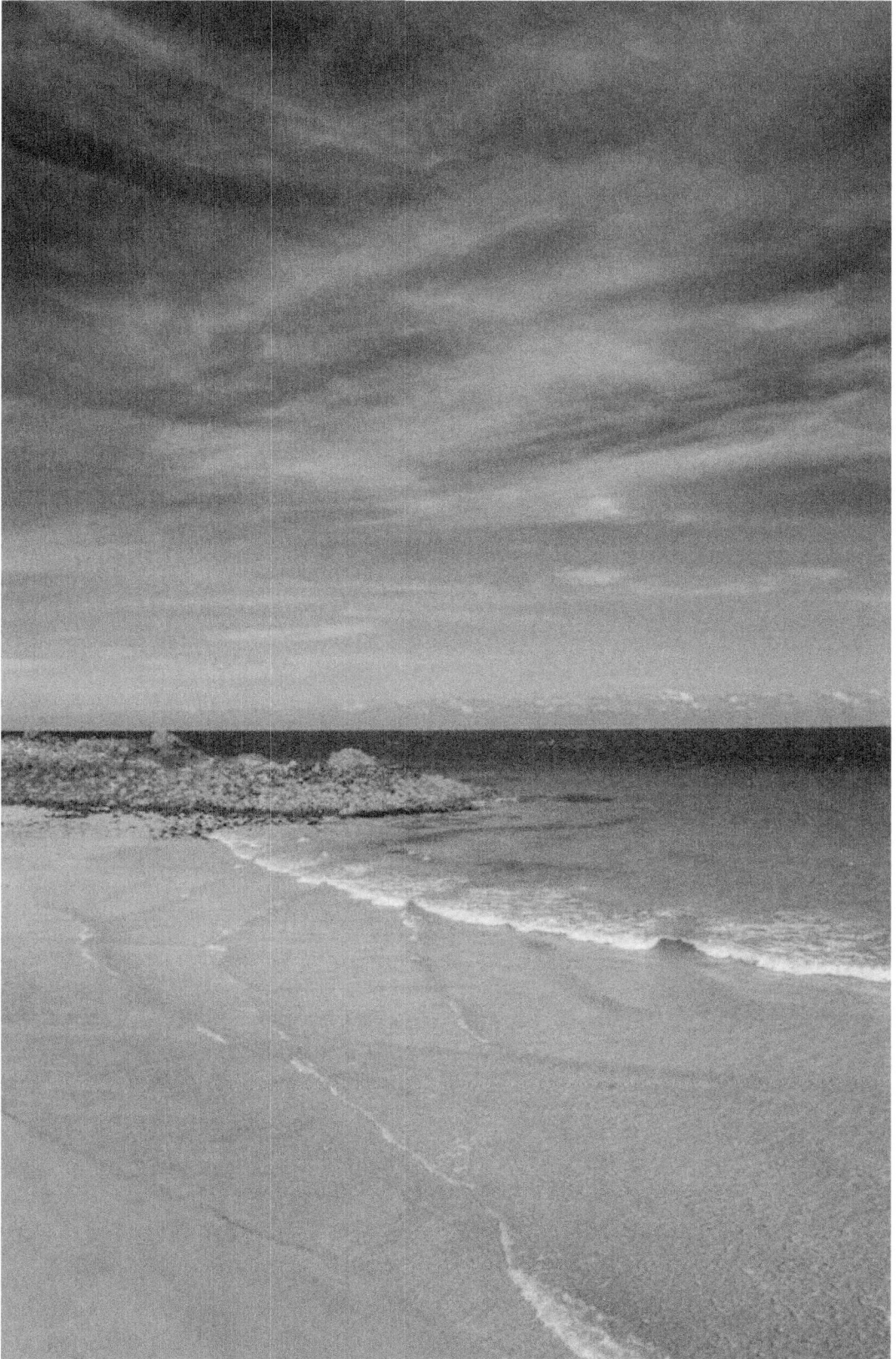

The Taste Of My Mother

The first thing that captured me was the aroma,

the scent of freshly cut bananas,

coffee, and sweet butter cake,

reminding me of childhood.

I remember those days so clearly,

sitting around the dining room table,

mouth full and warm, swollen tummy,

a taste of my mother still lingers in my breath.

Sweet and tangy, ripe and luscious,

plump and fertile,

the flavor lingers in my mouth,

bringing back this forgotten tenderness,

I combust.

Summer

I cherish summer like pancakes,

morning kisses and a warm cup of coffee.

Its warmth, sunshine,

longer nights by the ocean,

and the scent of salt and sea.

Lunar Glow

Beneath the navy blue expanse,

Devoid of stars, devoid of moons,

Lies a hypnotic darkness, profound.

I ponder if I could ascend and suspend,

A solitary light, the one that gleams,

Becoming the enigma of this night's shroud.

My eyes, like orbs of gold,

Like an owl, keen and watchful,

Vigilant over life's restlessness.

Embracing this utter obscurity,

The living essence of an earthly child.

Perhaps tonight is the night,

Where timid stars shed their fear,

And their radiance bathes me whole.

Let them cleanse my tainted flesh,

Let the earth's soil warm my skin,

I want to unleash my magic,

Reviving the lifeless,

Welcoming the forgotten,

Reborn in love.

Alma

Within the wild of the mountain woods,

Where rivers endlessly flow over pebbles,

Winds fiercely clash with the towering pines,

And colorful wildflowers paint the landscape,

While clouds and sunbeams

play a game of hide and seek,

I lie beneath time-honored pines,

My mind merging with the world around me,

Attuned to the voice of the wild wind,

Allowing my thoughts to roam freely,

This wilderness speaks with a mysterious voice,

Only in quietude can one grasp the woods' call.

I open my eyes, feeling free,

Like I could touch the clouds above

And melt into the sky so blue,

Glide like mist through the wildwood.

Everything moves and breathes,

These mountains teach me how to live.

The plants burst into bloom this time of year,

The streams never stop gently humming,

Life pulses around, vibrant and alive,

As the day softly fades away,

The full moon greets the untamed,

Its silver light shining through all.

I feel as one among this wild,

This is God's gift.

Earth Child

I embrace the night

as a child of twilight,

owls, fireflies, nymphs, and stars.

In darkness,

my wild takes flight,

I blend best in blackness,

afar from sight.

Wild Lavender

I'm a wild thing,

like lavender in lonely fields,

casting a lilac hue on everything,

breathing, alive.

Letting the sunbeam radiate within,

so that at night,

I can be the light within darkness,

surrounded by night creatures.

I've enjoyed living untied, free,

unburdened, and real.

Let my scent bring awakening and vibrancy.

Let my hues blend with life,

crafting a canvas for the wild and alive.

Wild woman dances,

night creatures in moonlit trance,

magic echoes rise.

Contrasts

I'm a paradox,

tough and tender,

ancient yet beautiful,

undangerously dangerous,

A constant mess of opposites,

I confess—How do I grow soft,

get old, call it enough?

Let me stand bare, ripe, and succulent,

so those who taste me may discover,

birthing me anew with each taste,

as if I were love—

Pure love.

New Beginning

Let me unleash a scream,

into the vast, black void,

where words float within gravity's force.

Let them pierce everything they touch,

a cry for help or relief

for those in pain.

Let the sound flow through you,

like blood through veins,

or thoughts toward parted lips.

It's all secure now,

just take that breath,

and release it all.

Let's begin anew.

Breath Of The Earth

The soil speaks to us in kindness,

Blooming words of sprouts and seeds.

Nature has a way with language,

Trees grow vertical to feel the sun closer,

Bees hum their breath

As they float over all that is vibrant,

Performing their morning dance.

Nothing seems to stand in the way of life,

Even the dead return so tenderly

To teach us that everything has its purpose.

Life has a way of tricking us

Into believing that there is some sort of end,

Just so it can all begin again,

And here I stand barefoot on our earth,

Taking it all in, like a big gulp of air,

Allowing it to flow as if it were my own blood.

This is how newness is born,

If you let it.

Cosmic Metamorphosis

As the night turns black,

I recall nights preceding this one,

each adorned with stars shinning bright,

illuminating the darkness within.

Today, all is dark, pure blackness,

yet, I'm content without light,

thriving in the midst of darkness.

You see, I'm the cosmos,

and darkness is my light.

You're the stars that brighten my galaxy,

and when all is black, it reminds me

of what existed before you,

and how you forever and infinitely

altered my perspective.

Ink-stained confession,

verse and grit collide fiercely,

poetry's raw roar.

Many Roles

From childhood to motherhood,

joy and strife, I've been it all—

daughter, friend, lover, worker in life.

Wife, manager, chasing dreams, no easy cure,

laughed hard, cried deep, each year a different lure.

With a writer's pen, embracing good and bad,

so many roles played, yet more to be had.

In this journey of living, when's the final call?

Living's tough; sometimes dying feels

like a soft fall.

Ready to stop pretending, one more role to shed,

let it be authenticity, the real me ahead.

To rest in comfort of that genuine role,

live fully or perish; that's my soul's goal.

Poppies

In a field painted with poppies,

I recline, embracing earth's softness

'neath the warming sky.

A landscape crimson, no need for more,

an exit wound where oneness and I commence.

A gift, mere existence,

bound with all that breathes,

wild and free, amidst the pulse of living things.

Brightest Darkness

A star hangs in the darkest

recesses of the universe,

Like a photon, a silver tear blazing,

A spectacle to behold.

The darkness surrounding it,

Macabre yet beautiful,

Sometimes, it is in this blackness

That light shines brightest.

Missing Winter

Birds sing all year,

didn't think I'd miss winter's chill,

bitting cold, quiet glory,

all dressed in white.

Here, it's endless spring,

some say paradise, I say home.

Ocean and mountains embrace,

daily nature uplifts the soul.

Maybe I'll revisit winter's magic,

someday soon.

Ocean's Call

The ocean dissolves its blues,

waves ebb with white frost,

blending effortlessly.

Smells like salt, sand, seashells,

let me sit on the wet sand,

the ocean won't mind,

let my lungs breathe salty wind

without the burn.

Feel like a pebble,

absorb it all,

wash me away,

blend me in.

I'm Enough

I need to remind myself often

that I am enough,

and let my voice wander

to the concealed spaces

where I can truly be me,

perfectly imperfect,

an open soul

letting the sun

radiate my light,

open,

honest,

naked.

Green Remains

I've heard before

That nothing green can stay,

But here on this island,

Green is the only color

That truly remains.

I've become acquainted

With this perpetual blooming,

The endless season of spring.

As I stand firm on this new land

And watch each sunrise and sunset pass,

I wonder if the season will ever shift,

If this green will ever fade.

In this ceaseless bloom,

I uncover who I once lost,

I'm reborn.

About Trees

I often wonder about trees,

And their turning bodies,

Reaching high towards the light,

Always standing

Over sun or snow,

While making soft murmurs

To the wind, their voice.

I often wonder

How many seasons

They have lived through,

From swelling with buds

To shedding their leaves

As if they lost their coats

When they needed them most,

During the cold.

How they never rest,

Yet never grow tired,

Only grow stronger, taller, wiser.

I wish I were more like a tree,

And less like a human,

Allowing the rain to be shared

Between me and the other living things,

Allowing the sun to kiss me,

And the seasons to change me,

Always growing stronger,

Always humbled, unhurried,

Just a tree.

Shoreline's Love

The ocean is tranquil this morning,

Liquid cobalt waters rest under the sky

While the sunbeams cast a golden glow.

What a spectacle to watch!

Near the shoreline,

The air breathes of salty shells,

The waves, gifted painters,

Leave foamy strokes in the sand

For the tide to kiss later.

Its voice rumbles, yet gentle,

A soft cry that rouses the gulls,

Inviting them to greet the day.

Yet the shore is in love with its depth,

And awaits the waters' love in return.

Ever-expanding Mind

I'm curious about the universe,

How it never ceases to expand,

How it never stays the same,

Always grows within darkness,

creating beautiful, glittery

things that shine so pretty.

I want my mind to mirror it,

To never cease to amplify,

So that I can use it to create art,

And write the most beautiful

poetry for you to read.

Supernova

I've heard this June

all planets will align,

It's a rare occurrence,

Almost never occurs.

It seems the moods are based

by all that's planetary.

My mind feels this divine pull,

Like a black hole

drawing inspiration inward.

There is a constant

cosmic storm brewing within,

a quasar illuminating my thoughts.

The truth is—I'm afraid,

Like a supernova I might burst and fade,

How I wish I could contain my brilliance,

like a star in the night sky

And not be influenced by this energy pull

Which drives me into pure madness.

Missing You

The woods softly call me once more.

That cabin by the river's edge

Longs for my presence,

So I can wander through the snowy forest

As I did years past, in cold and darkness.

The moose keep returning,

As if they held secrets untold.

The frozen river never thaws completely,

Always dark, damp, and treacherous.

I could return, but things have changed,

Life is harder; it all feels distant now.

Maybe this call will fade over time,

As I sit, graying in my new home.

Instead, I'll dream of you and miss you.

Stubborn

As the aspen trees turned gold,

and the pine trees browned,

the ivy remained green

all year long.

So stubborn,

trying to remain the same

while everything else changed.

Pouring Rain

I yearn to dance in the rain,

The one that pours,

that makes its song

as water droplets

kiss the waiting earth.

I'll sip from the heavens,

bathe in its grace,

allow it to fill me whole,

like a wet embrace,

creating puddles

for kids to play.

I feel this sense of peace

when I'm in its embrace,

as if it washed my sins

and made me pure

again and again.

As if it were able to erase

all sad memories

with its tears,

making me feel wholly

once more.

Nature's Awakening

The sunrise, it's different here,

A soft fawn, so delicate,

Like floral scents saturating

The sunshine with a pale light.

The sea looks back with its calm waves,

And the gulls dressing in white

Sing their hollow cries in the air.

It's as magical as kissing the stark sand,

Everything in glow births like earth's miracle,

Softly warming all that's alive.

My Muse, My Love

2

I have been both loved and lonely,

it just depends on the season.

It Was Always You

In the midst of it all,

it was always you.

Our eyes searching

For each other,

our lips nourishing

one another.

It was always you.

Our hands warming

our bodies,

and our words healing

Our souls.

Love You Always

I remember

when you held me

when my body wouldn't,

and how your lips

nourished me

when mine no longer would,

and I love you for that.

Hunger

I know now,

It was all for hunger.

The insatiable need for more.

Deep down, I knew all along

that you would kill for this,

and I wanted that—you to do it.

You asked to touch me,

and I wanted to feel alive.

After all, we both needed us,

a surrender that kept us humble,

giving this flesh what it craved,

as you begged, "Don't leave too soon."

Uninhibited Flames

I feel quite dim,

Yet with you, I'll shine.

You ignite my fire,

Turn me to flame.

Together, we'll tend to our wounds,

Mending our souls' residue

With uninhibited laughter,

We'll let our light drift,

Then return to earth,

With our souls crowned.

And I miss everything about you,

your smell, touch, smile

and friendship, but above all,

your kindness.

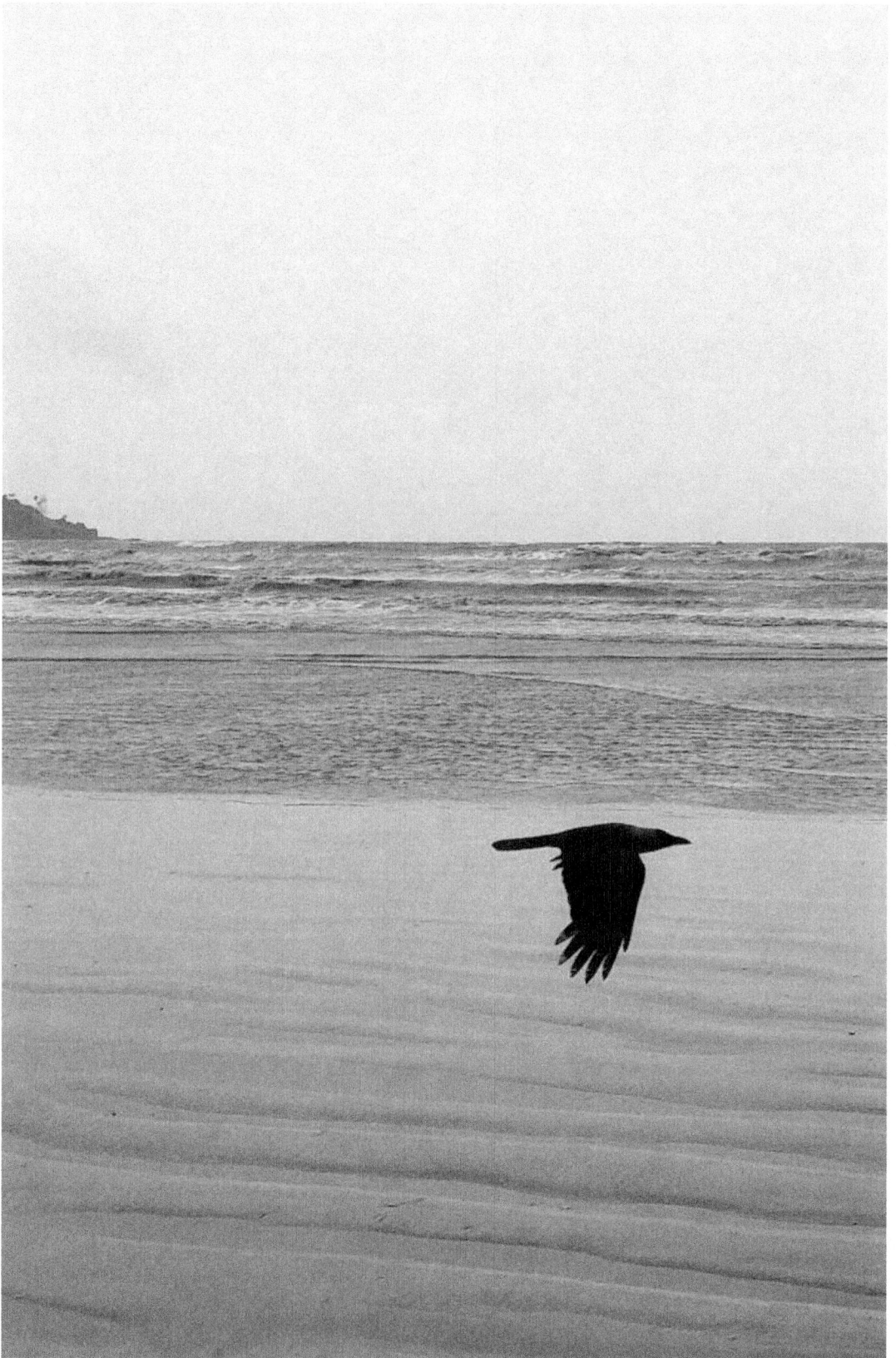

Once More

Soon, another time comes,

we say our goodbyes.

Love, like a changing poem,

shaped by our making.

Lips, soft comfort, wanting more.

I'll miss you near,

long days and nights,

until you're back.

I'll wait here,

love graying,

true, I know.

Words I've Sown

I'm naked,

I stand exposed,

stripped of pretense,

clothed only in the words I've sown.

I bear myself open and true,

I yearn for you to feel me as I feel you.

Starting With You

Someone told me to choose things

That I'm willing to live for and fully love,

And that happiness will follow.

So I started with you,

Because you're my favorite thing,

And I love you wholly and purely.

Now, I hope to live happily ever after.

Soft

As I grow old,

I see love as this softness,

almost as if it were this kind thing

that envelops two hearts with passion.

A fire so soft that only burns

if it exists its heart ventricle,

a love so kind that only becomes angry

if it is made to not last.

Your arms make me feel

Cozy as a bud tucked tight,

Like a firefly in a moonlit jar,

Warm and glowing.

My New Heaven

Waking up to sandy hair,

seashells and salty skin,

feels akin to waking up to your kisses,

in moments when you are distant.

This is my new haven.

Youth's Philosophy

I remember years past,

When I was in my twenties,

Plumped with youth and passion,

You had my heart in your mouth,

Your loving was merciless,

Leaving me trembling.

Eye against eye,

breath wanting breath.

My hungry, pretty body

Always wanted more of you,

And you, never wanted to miss me,

Not one day; we were all we had.

Mash Potatoes

I want to be soft

like mashed potatoes,

I want my taste to be remembered

as pliable and mendable.

Life has made a version of me

that is too hard.

I want to live just one day

mushy and gentle,

so you can taste the one

you once loved.

Choosing You

Time has taught me this about love:

It's more than just a feeling;

it's a promise to stay.

If you wonder why I'm here with you,

it's not that I can't love another body,

or that my pupils can't find another attractive.

I could love many seasons,

paint with countless colors,

find joy in the sun as much as the rain,

and be pleased by someone else's touch.

Yet, I simply choose not to.

You've deeply etched

your mark within my being.

That, in itself, is ample.

You are ample.

Eyes Of The Unseen

Your eyes, vessels of truth,

Like sacred pools of holy water,

Imbuing your existence

While mirroring the wonder

Of all that is beautiful.

Your tears, like liquid glass,

Endlessly vast and transparent,

A see-through window of you.

Peel my layers with your glance,

Expose impurities or falsehoods,

Share your honest soul with me,

Let them captivate my core,

Making me your own.

Sweet And Sticky

In the oven is the banana bread,

seasoned with cut almonds and honey,

three thick slices freshly cut,

ready for us to share with warm chamomile tea.

My love shall taste the sweetest of pieces;

let me add a bit more honey

to sweeten the bite,

holding it between his fingers,

putting it in his mouth,

it melts his heart with memories

of comfort... so sticky,

such sweet bread is loving and caring,

and makes a tummy full and happy.

Slow Love

Love took longer than usual to be felt,

It had to be slow, soft, but mostly kind,

That was most important.

There are chapters that are better closed,

So later, they can be reopened

To see what changed.

I want to stop wondering if we are real,

And simply live knowing that we matter,

At least to one another.

Wake up to the warming of the sun,

Embrace your body,

and take it all in.

Begging Soft

Begging voices, soft and near,

Longing for a sign to show,

Our bodies sweat and moan.

In empty hearts, we find our fear,

Craving what we hold most dear.

Dive into this silent space,

Kiss the quiet, set it free,

In this moment, you and me,

Together, we'll meet face to face.

Scars Of Love

Love always left

the ugliest of scars,

protruding and thick,

filled with intertwined fibers

that reminded those who saw,

the grief hidden beneath the skin.

Leaving healing marks,

so you could retrace

the cruelty that gently

mended each wound.

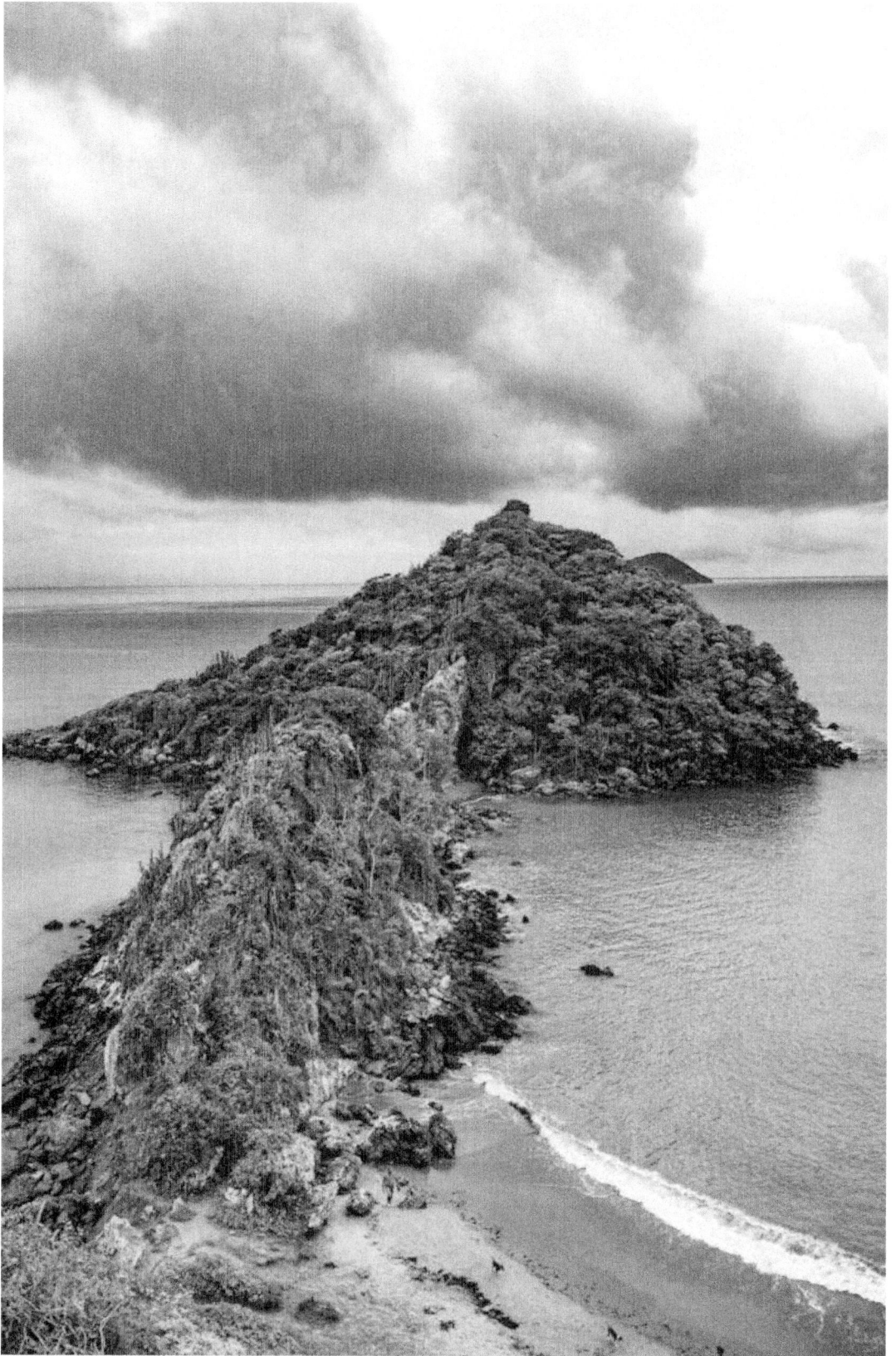

Love's Gravity

In the moon's softer glow,

And the stars' relentless shine,

My love for you, a force to expand,

In your arms, I can't decline.

I can't resist, I can't refrain,

Powerless against this pull.

With you, my heart's on fire, full.

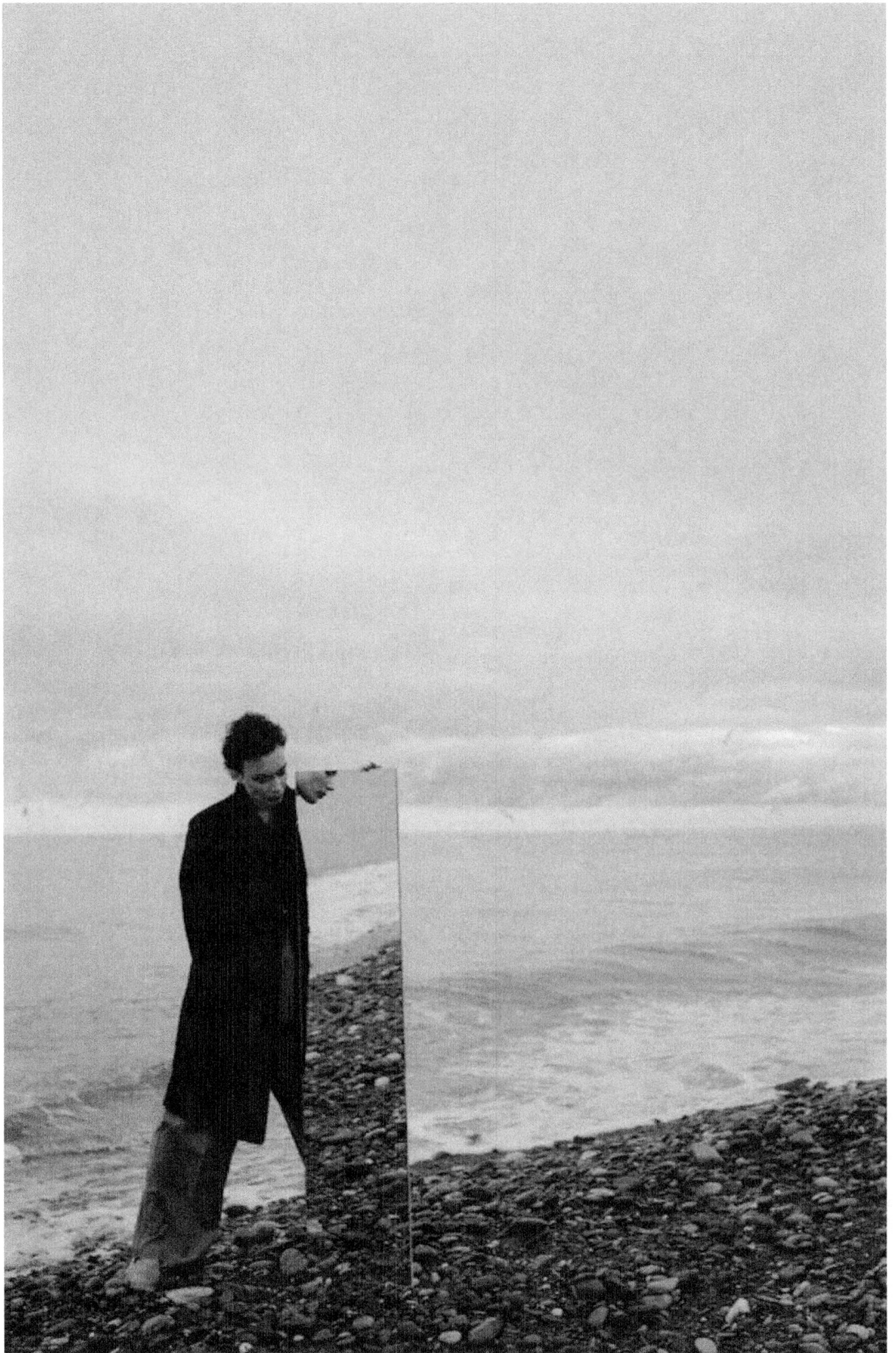

I've ever known that loving you

demands to still this abyss.

In that space, there's no room

for both love and void.

Love's Sinews

Our love is bound in sinews,

Deep as marrow within bones,

Lips, skin, breath merge as one,

Entangling our very souls.

Soon, our eyes will meet again,

Hands tracing each familiar curve,

Voices confessing sins once more,

You and I, as always, will lie,

As if time had never passed.

Allow me to unwrap you,

As you become my miracle,

Let me be your opus,

We burn and turn,

As bones turn to ash.

Love Hungry

I hunger for love,

not just any love.

I crave the kind

that keeps you alive,

the sort that leaves

your thirst unquenchable.

I need it to be

soft and wild,

I need it to burn,

for burning me well

is better than feeling

nothing at all.

I ache to be consumed by it.

I love you wholly,

every version of you,

no judgements,

no expectations,

just all of you

Scented You

How fresh your scent of primroses,

Like spring in May,

The fragrance of rain and dew—

Everything reminds me of you.

Now, as I come of age,

I bloom beside you still,

Imbuing what's left of my youth.

I've lived and written many lives,

All with you by my side.

Each verse, a scent, a flower,

You are but a bloom

That keeps on dying and living,

Just so I can breathe you in deeply

And write of all the beauty in you.

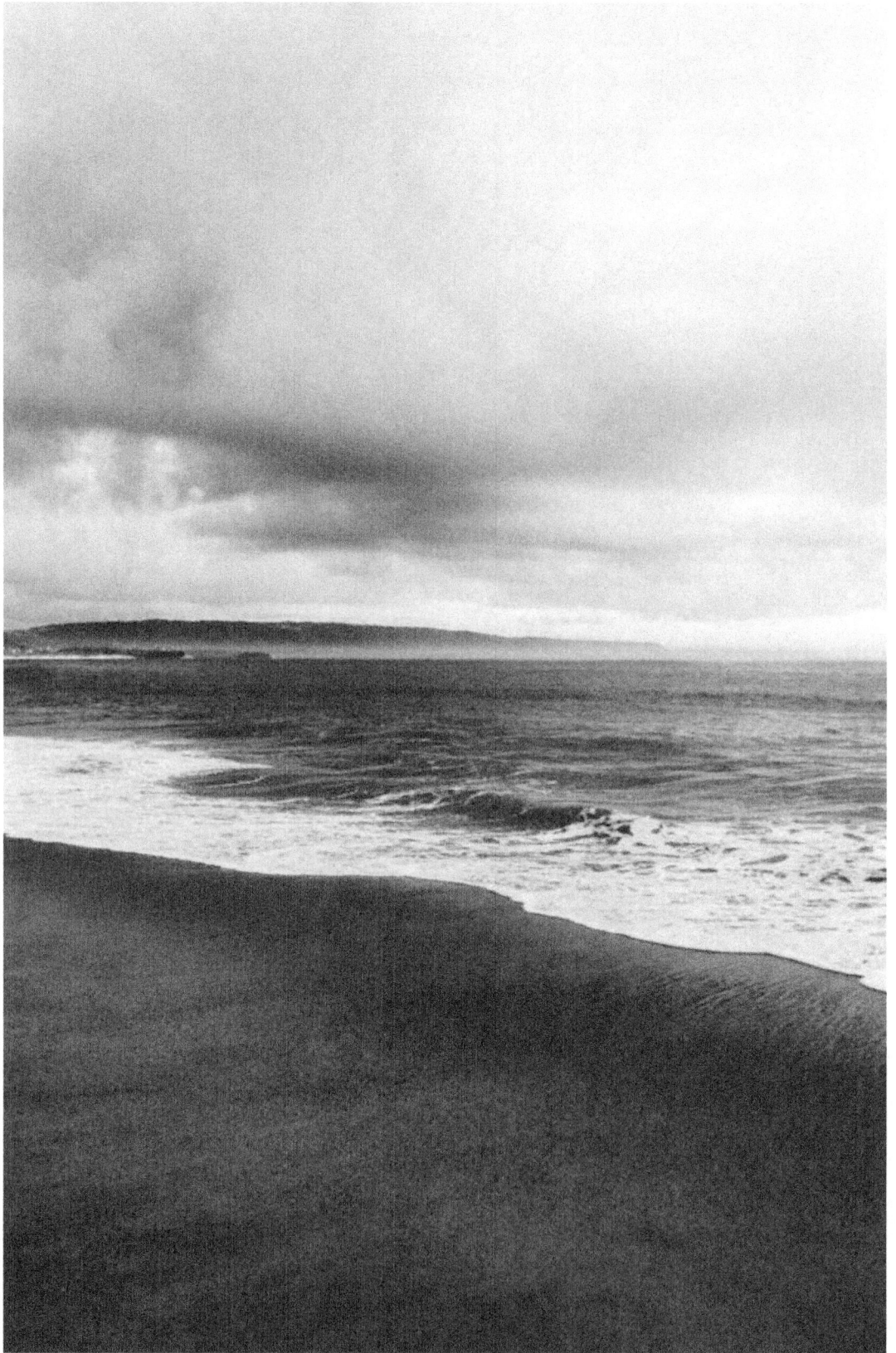

Choosing Our Best Pieces

Perhaps we only offer fragments of ourselves,

But choosing our best pieces to share is an art.

After all, giving away all that we are,

In the end might cause more grief

Than if we only pick and choose what to share.

I've mastered this art quite well,

But I did give you the best of me.

Flaws & Love

I'll always remember

When I lay naked beside you

And shared every scar on my body,

How each fiber intertwined painfully

While telling its own vulnerable story,

And your fingers traced over each imperfection,

Admiring every contour of each mark,

As you leaned close to my right ear

And whispered so softly—'I love you whole.'

That meant more to me than us making love.

Mossy Green Shame

My fresh thoughts, unburied,

encased within your heart,

I got lost in your eyes,

A mossy green shame.

I feel it's all my fault,

So I'll bear all the blame.

Assist me to breathe,

Savor my life's remnants.

Entomb me in shame,

Taste the brine of my nest,

Conceal my wounds,

Let the sunbeams console my burns.

I tried hard for a husband,

But instead I got a distant friend.

Bruises carved on my heart,

I never was like them.

Fire And Ash

You wear those eyes well,

Deep in the soul,

Like watercolor, soft yet fierce.

I remember your first glance,

A fire's rampage,

Leaving only ashes,

All grey softness.

Now, my heart is yours.

Graying

How I wish I could hold you near,

Feel your heartbeat against mine.

It's been too long, my dear.

Sometimes your memory fades,

And I have to dive deep inside

To revive it, and feel it again.

I'll sit here graying, missing you.

Satiating Hunger

This tension feeds me,

But I never cease being hungry.

We feed off of each other,

Losing eyesight for one another,

Maybe this passion satiates my ravenousness.

Feed me words between the lines

That may comfort me,

Hold me tight, exhume my fears,

Let me vanish in your soulful poetry.

I want to bleed out my endorphins

And share them with your soul's depth

To release all this strain that separates us.

Let me be yours only, forever,

And you will be mine, become my angel.

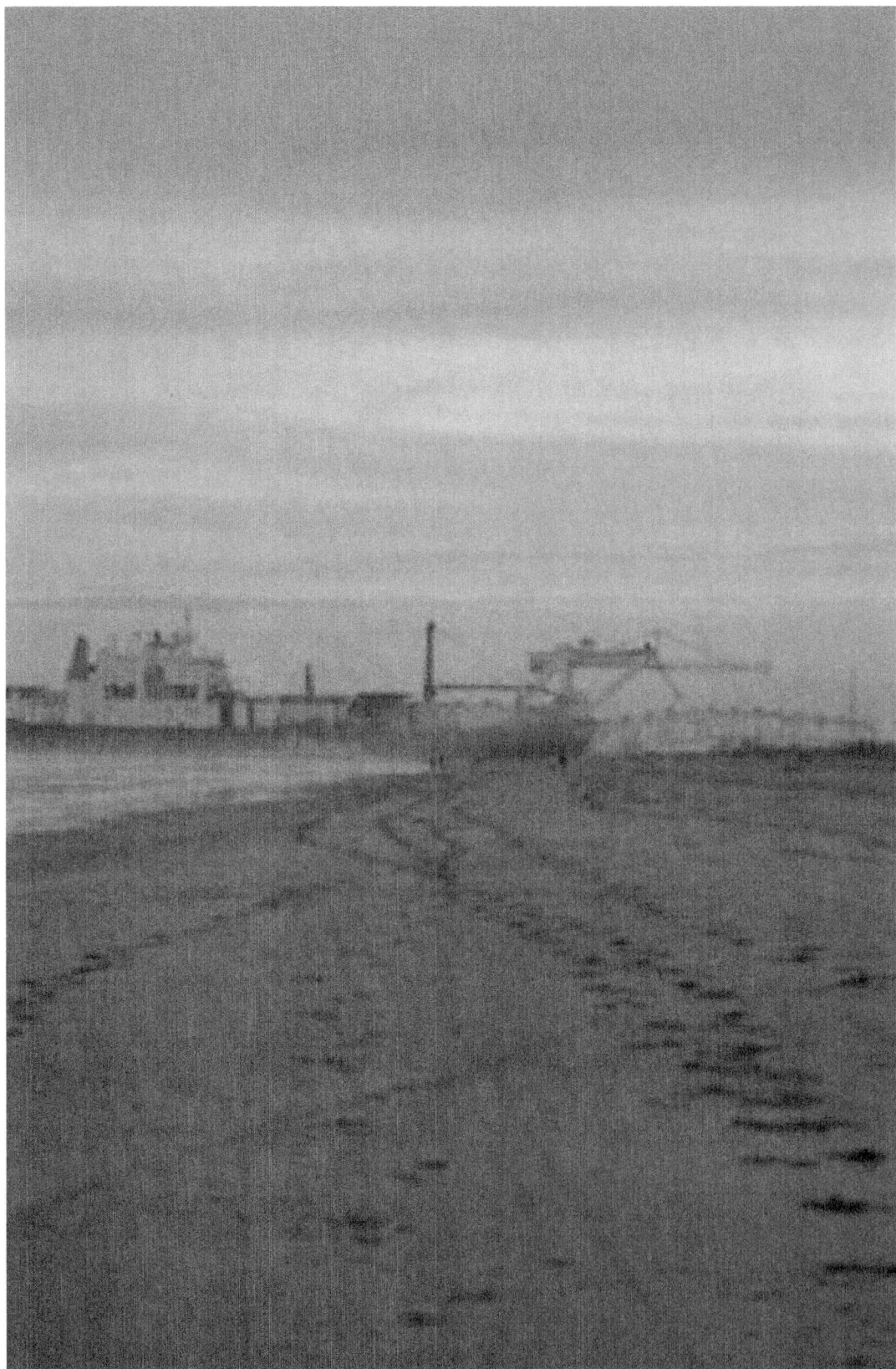

Day's Start

Morning sun sneaks through,

warming the day's start.

I want to capture its magic,

a warm coffee cup,

a toast filled with butter.

All this peaceful—emptiness.

I seek happiness in these moments,

when you're not here to share

this everyday beauty.

Perhaps sharing a fragment

of all I feel now,

what I can't share...

All I crave right now, you.

Seeping Souls

I want to allow my nakedness

To seep through me onto you,

So we can be as one.

This pure wildness,

That is fully enough.

Life Is Hard

3

My ribcage expands and swallows

the grief I inhaled so deeply.

Set It On Fire

I confess there are days I crave

some warmth to hug me,

a heat that ignites me on fire

like incandescent coal,

that keeps me burning

as if I was sort of celestial.

I want to flare up the love within,

seize this heat by sharing of it,

allowing miracles to radiate,

as if I were an angel aflame,

bestowing this fire

to turn all that is dead or sad

into luminous flames of kindness.

My Madness

Madness has a way to spread

Like wildfire through a dry forest.

It takes root like ivy on an old wall

And it swarms like bees from a disturbed hive.

Like a dark cave, it traps you in its depths,

A fog, obscuring your thoughts and vision,

Lurking in the corners of your mind.

I know this because I've lived it,

I know this because I'm mad.

Odd Number

I'm the odd number,

the weird and bold amid the strange,

Let me find those who shine brightest

among the unruly, with unwritten fate.

I want to find my way around this world

and change it with a new theme of love.

Let's make revolution of the strange,

let us all rise from the ashes,

we, the weirdest.

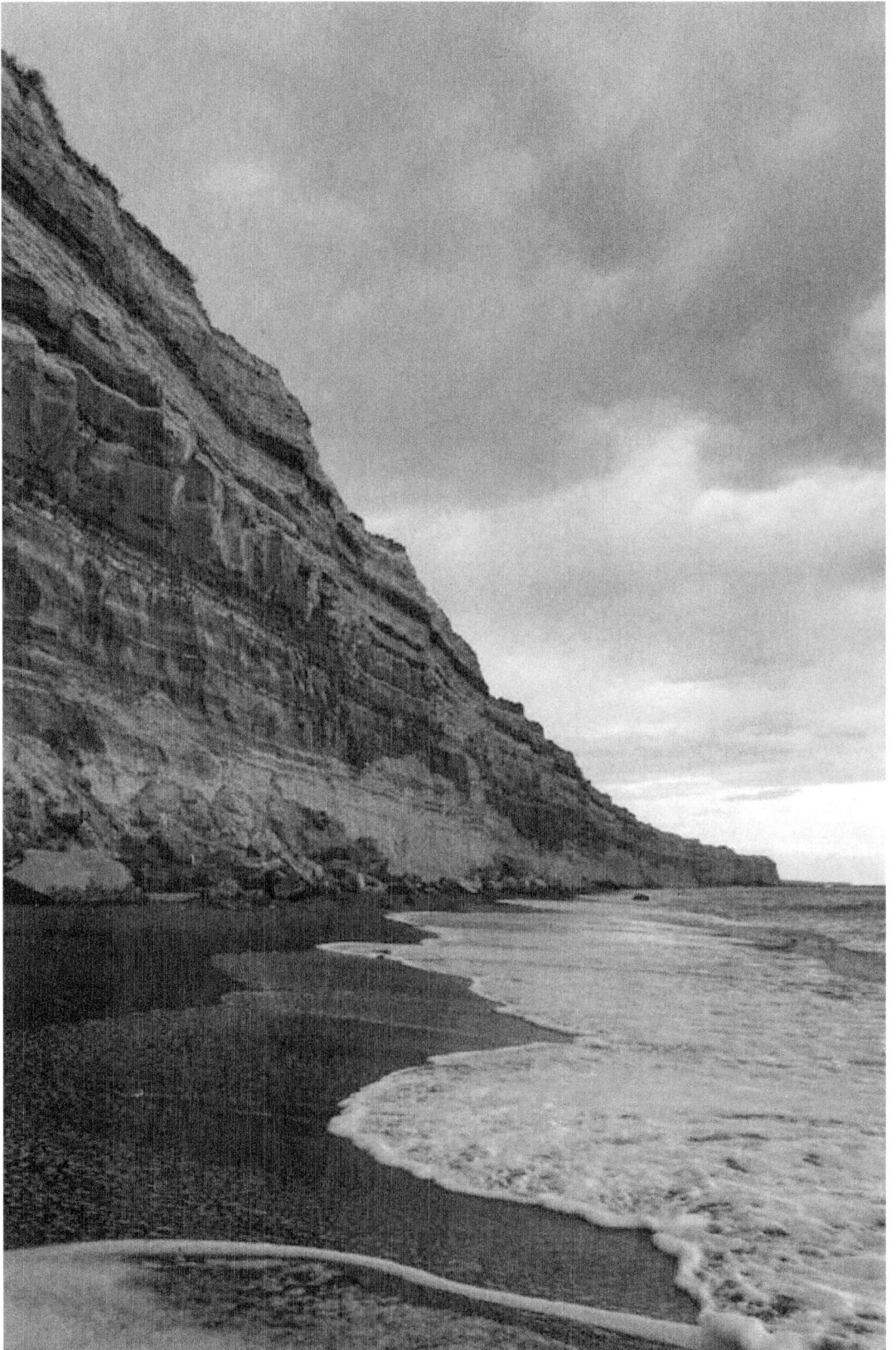

The Artistry Of Sorrow

There's art in crying,

I've grown quite adept at it,

letting tears fill my eyes

for it feels good at times.

Strength I find in the tears,

relief from what's awry.

I seem to master this art,

dad dubbed me theatrical,

now, here as a poet,

perhaps he was right, after all.

I craft tales for belief, a wound that won't heal,

sawdust, ashes, and dirt, nothing more remains.

Skilled at making things pretty,

driving men to madness,

"Burn me further, till naught is left".

When will this fragile body

lay to rest and learn to accept

that slow days are the way

to heal and bloom

not just a way to unwind.

Behind Close Doors

Sorrow lurks behind closed doors,

A pain that gutted me whole.

Some days,

I feel your love lingering

As it once did.

Yet others,

I struggle to shake this feeling.

A numbness burrows deeper,

Creating a void within.

I feel as though

I've become soulless

Layers Of Forty Six

I woke up once again, one more day to live,

trying to come to terms with it,

as if it weren't a miracle to see my face

again in the cloudy mirror.

I'm just about to turn forty six.

I feel it's been forty six long years

that keep peeling off layers

from the skin to my organs,

allowing my sour to surface

from all I've lived and left.

Throughout the day, my thoughts wander

to when I might fade, yet time relentlessly passes

—one more minute, another year.

I want time to unwrap

the remaining goodness in me,

but perhaps all that lingers

is this flesh and bones.

Years past, I was this soft-spoken woman

with big, full passionate heart,

full of kindness, full of life.

Now, I am just empty bones,

nothing left to be shared.

Untamed Moment

I was born starving,

craving the unfathomable.

Longing for love's return

in a world estranged.

Aching for breath, existence,

and laughter unrestrained.

Born hungry,

a force devouring lifeless.

Now, my hunger perished,

yearning for life's raw essence.

I want to feel the unfelt

and live when I gave up on living.

In the tight space

between ribcage and heart, I hide,

a dormant seed awaiting

the untamed moment to ignite.

Vacant Heaven

I've been praying to God,

But the heavens are voiceless,

No answers ever come,

And I'm left with silence.

Perhaps I must find my own way,

Trusting in the strength of my own steps,

Yet I have scars on my feet,

from the roads I've walked.

Pardon my faith against the lies.

Cloaked In Grief

Grief came so soon,

Like a heavy cloak,

wrapping all in sorrow.

Mind and heart veiled,

Its pain, a phantom limb,

a constant reminder of what is missing.

Stop time, this feeling still lingers,

This agony has swallowed me whole.

I gaze upon the starry night,

But all I find is stark darkness.

Perhaps the moon will grace us tomorrow,

Illuminating the night,

And carrying away this affliction.

Pill By Pill

Doctors tend to overprescribe,

A pill for this,

A pill for that.

I keep taking those damn pills,

With no one heeding the alarming fallout.

By the time the doctors see the damage,

I've already dug my own grave.

Pill after pill leads to my decay.

Just one more pill—

To claim yet another soul fragment,

Till naught remains.

Just me, my grave,

And those damn pills.

Seed Of Renewal

In the quiet descent of golden leaves,

Darkness encroaches, as evening grieves.

Sterile soil longs for a green hue,

Beneath naked trees, where blooms once grew.

Rivers dry, desolate shores,

Life gives in to death's harsh grip,

Yet within sharp cries, a hushed flight,

As rivers awaken, reclaiming their strength.

"I return," they cry,

As wind sows seeds with tender care.

Rain softly weeps, soil to soak,

There is hope to be tasted,

A cycle is reborn.

Fractured Plumes

Can angels reside with flesh and bones,

Crooning to us songs of love.

Can they meet demise by self-inflicted fate?

Can they mourn their mourning

And live their living while we all sleep?

There is a window in his eyes,

Blue galaxies that stare deeply.

There is meaningless meaning

In each word spoken,

Disorderly discord exists within the mouth.

Slay me with your rage and sadness,

Let me heal your brokenness, madness.

Let me mend your fractured plumes

So you can fly to heaven and wait there for me.

Urban Tide

The ocean hungers for emotions raw,

Feelings pure, flowing as waves roar.

But around it, poison holds dominion,

City's fumes mute its voice.

It craves a soul untamed,

To stir its depths, unashamed.

Rain, salty tears, to cleanse its shore,

From city's grip, it longs to rise.

In empty streets, dead souls wander,

Sewage spills, all life's anguish.

Yearning for a cleanse, a healing,

From this despair, it cries for air.

Becoming

Let me mourn,

let me grieve,

let me be.

I want to be whole.

Let the sun soften me

with its warmth.

Open my ribs

and release this pain.

Make me into something beautiful.

Blood Red Tulips

When I die,

place fresh red tulips upon my grave
to recall all the passion that forged me.
Let their roots caress my tomb so softly,
Ensure they gleam as brightly as blood
And dress resplendently in red.

I want my fervor to be borne
across my form, across yours.

Lucifer

Some days, I call to Lucifer,

Today's one of those damn days.

Too warm, too naive; wolves devour me.

Once thought I was a miracle,

Now just an accident.

Prayed to God, learned it's false.

Constantly trapped in barbed wire,

Can't break away.

Can't distinguish white from grey,

All the same shame.

Scared of myself,

Lost in blackness,

Like crows on rotten flesh.

Maybe the devil hears,

Why do I lie to myself?

Immersing In Tragedy

Maybe it is in tragedy

That we find our finest ideas.

Our minds shift to creativity

In order to heal all that pain,

And the best poetry emerges from it.

It's a painful, necessary experience

So you can find the depths of yourself,

And everyone feels your words more,

When they come from that sacred space.

Vanishing Act

I've held all this pain so deep,

I'm not who others think of me.

Life's sweetness has soured,

We both know, I must confess.

You know well what's going on,

No more tremors, no more fear.

I'm just the chemicals consumed,

A slave to the intoxicating haze,

Lost in the opiate's hypnotic smog.

Thoughts haphazardly strewn,

I knew this moment would soon loom,

But I don't want to change my ways.

So let me fade fast, I'll take flight.

I won't intrude upon your space,

I won't shadow you, my dear.

I'm well-acquainted with failure,

I'll seek solace far from here.

Time's Sip

Sitting in a cozy coffeehouse nook,

Slowly sipping hot chamomile brew,

Watching the clock, each minute runs,

Feeling as if I live on everyone's time.

This life distills the life of my being,

Exhausted, yet sleep evades me deep.

The clock ticks on, a relentless cue,

Sip and drink, no rush, no fuss.

Wishing I could live on my own time.

I scream, I hurt, this lie is too much,

So sip and drink, tick and clock,

No time to sigh while life deceives.

Calm Mindset

When I self-medicate,

I fall into rapture.

Medicine flows through me,

Releasing joy in my mind,

Healing every pain,

Worries vanish,

Leaving peace and warmth.

No more thoughts, just calm.

In this tranquil state,

The mind becomes quiet,

Thoughts arise and fade away.

No need to hold or chase,

Just let them come and go freely.

Paper Doll Facade

Altered digital renditions of your face,

Just knockoffs of paper dolls, fake.

Sculpted figures weep, caught in vulnerability,

Elicit joy in people's responses to your presence,

It's all just hypocrisy, all insincere.

Be angry at what all has become,

Be honest and smile.

It's all a game no one wants to play,

Yet all know too well, an emotional facade.

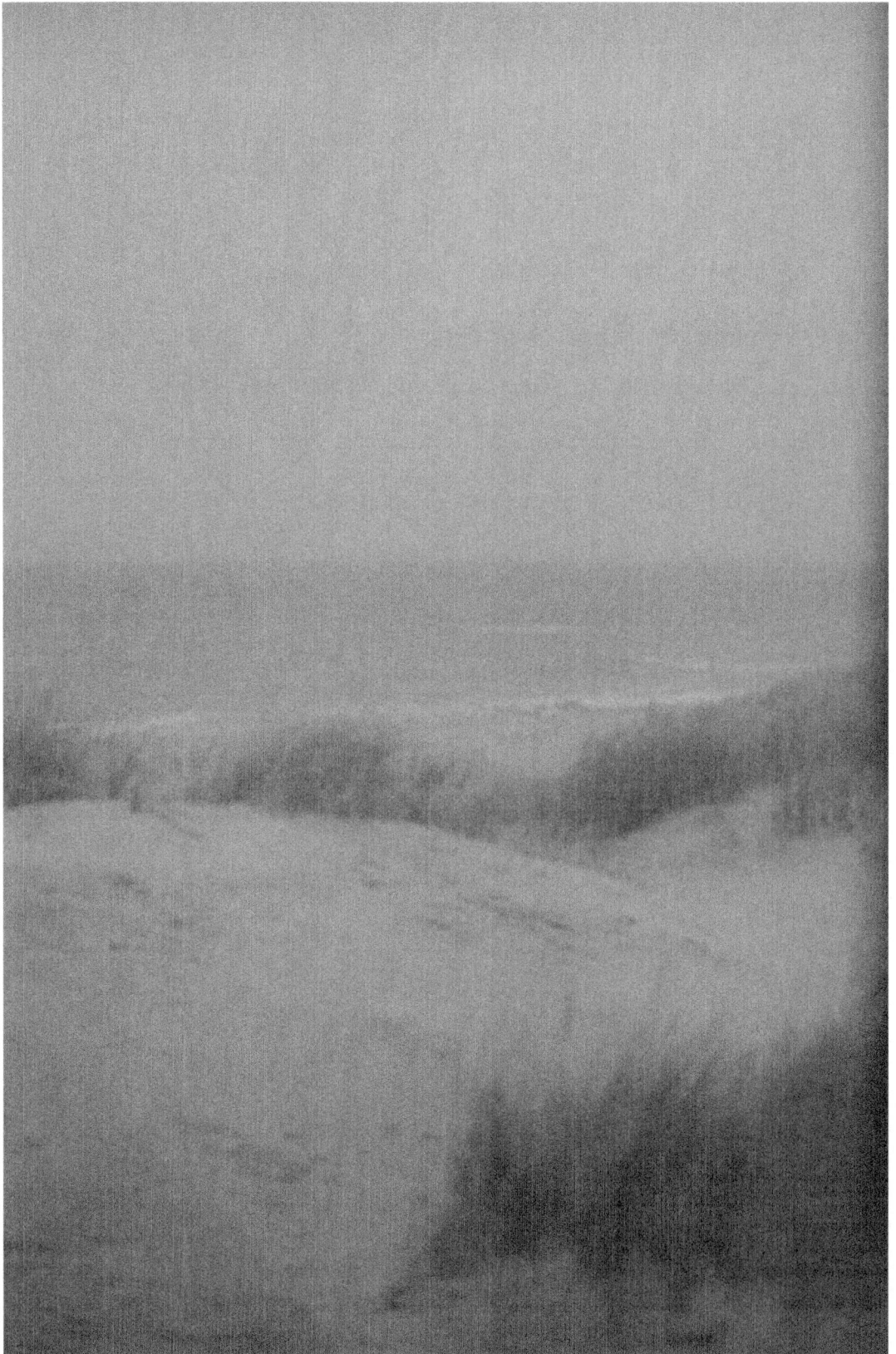

Tortured Existence

I wonder sometimes why living

Causes such torture.

They told me living was a gift,

As if it descended from the sky

And greeted you unasked for,

Yet for me, living is hard.

Each day, each passing minute,

Feels like this doom hanging

From my skull, crippling me,

Like a heavy weight on the lungs.

And I just want to breathe in this offering,

Yet I am unable to feel it as a blessing.

My ribcage is recreating itself

By inhaling oxygen and exhaling

what no longer serves

Dreaming Bird

The bird stopped calling this morning.

I wonder if it was a dream

or a vague memory

of his song now long gone.

I feel this silence

has brought a new storm,

so I will wait,

bring peace to me now.

Starkly Empty

I've pleaded with doctors

For numbness,

Pills that bring me to stillness.

I hear my husband's words daily;

He tells me to smile,

Smile some more, it will do you well,

Perhaps some sun will heal you.

His words stab through my skin

like gleaming needles,

Eradicating thoughts of

The empathy one should hold.

I sit in a corner, watching my words

Fade out of sight.

Sometimes it's not what one

thinks one should crave;

Maybe, all I want is to be starkly empty.

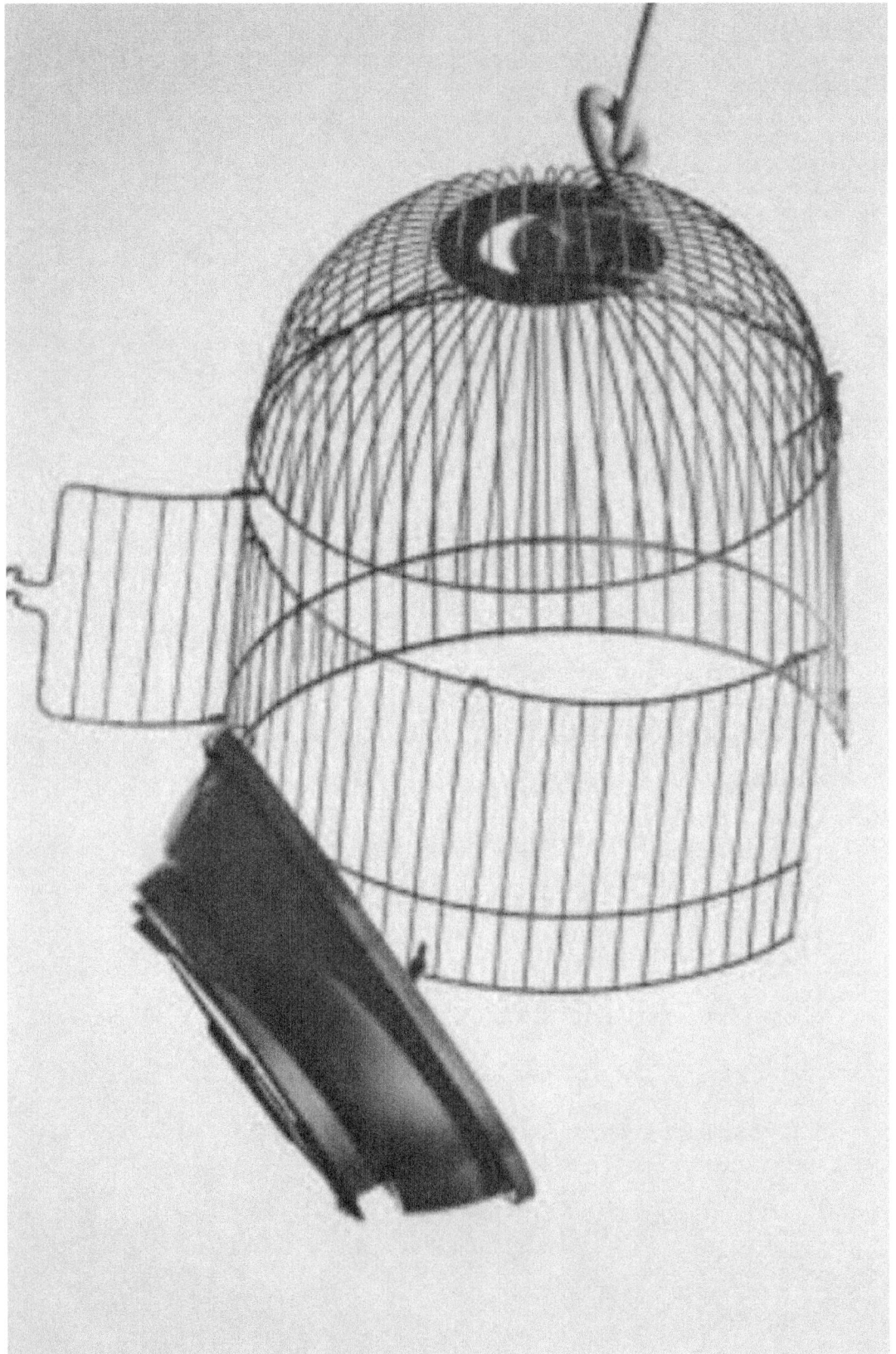

Skin Me

In the fading light as the sun sets low,

I may seem dim but I still shine some.

Skin my heart, let emotions stay shards,

Erase the sting, assist me to breathe,

Peel back the soul, let it drift, soar,

The day has ceased, It's time to rise.

Missed Signs

Some endeavor to deconstruct me,

As if I were a puzzle to untangle.

Essentially, I'm a poet,

Yet, at my core, mere secrets

For none to uncover.

Primarily a dreamer,

With feet aloft on the moon,

Thoughts that cling to the stars,

And music as my compass.

I revel in becoming ethereal,

Absorbing every sensation deeply,

Yet I'm just another tormented poet,

Holding onto emotion,

And deriving inspiration from the entirety.

Soaked In Black

The news, a weight heavier than quietus,

Feelings soaked in demise,

All fades to black.

I miss you, we miss you.

Blossoms left to wither,

Yet your soul's light holds steady.

Perhaps we'll meet where heaven kisses hell.

Teach me your sorrow's song,

Let my kisses dry your tears, my angel.

Let your wings unfurl and shake,

Reclaiming all that was clipped away.

I miss you, we miss you.

Burdened Bones

Growth is heavy,

a burden in the bones,

days where seeking help screams,

"I'm still here."

Better years, golden glory fades,

gone—nothing to nourish dry soil,

A heart, weathered and worn,

craving stories in whispers, bold.

Silent pleas pour through stillness,

I see my life unfold, like petals of old.

I surrender—a dance of moments, fleeting.

"I'm still here," this I know for sure,

Through the fertile, yet barren field.

Bloom struggles amid the dead.

Broken

Gutted, disemboweled

By your words, I lay.

I've kept crafting falsehoods

That we were okay.

The truth is, like diverging rivers,

our paths gently drifted away.

It's Not Easy Being Human

There was a time when

I would disappear within nature

Just as rain fades

When it kisses the earth.

Nature nourished me,

It held me in ways

My own body couldn't.

I remember getting lost

Between pine trees

And fields of poppies.

The smell of summer

Sun bathed me,

And it felt like happiness,

Everything was just right.

I want to hold on

To what is now gone.

I want to feel all that

I once felt, so deeply,

And allow it to turn me

Into what nourishes,

What is hungry.

Sometimes being human

Is harder than being

A scented flower,

Or a steady river that flows.

Allow me to be all that

I don't know how to be.

It's time to bloom.

Salty Water Eyes

My tears flow like waves on my lids

With a morbid fear gripping me,

That I may never see you again,

That I won't survive this separation,

I need you, I miss you.

My eyes turn into salt-fresh seawater.

The moon swells, big and fat,

Against the starry black sky.

I hold my breath, hoping to catch a glimpse of you,

While fearing my brain might suffocate.

But oh, my dear children thrive,

An anchor that keeps me here, that makes me stay.

These silly emotions deepen,

With a 'sorry' permeating my being,

Drowning me as if I orchestrated my own death.

This torrent of emotion slowly suffocates:

As if wasting my life were my daily routine.

Perhaps I'm just a bright dying moon,

And those who behold me

Witness my gradual decay.

Distilled Sappiness

I'm sappy, through and through,

My daily brew is laughter and tears.

Emotions swell, scalding hot,

Steeped like stinging, boiling tea,

Distilling all I have to imbue.

So here I stand, unabashedly me,

In a world of sappy dreams.

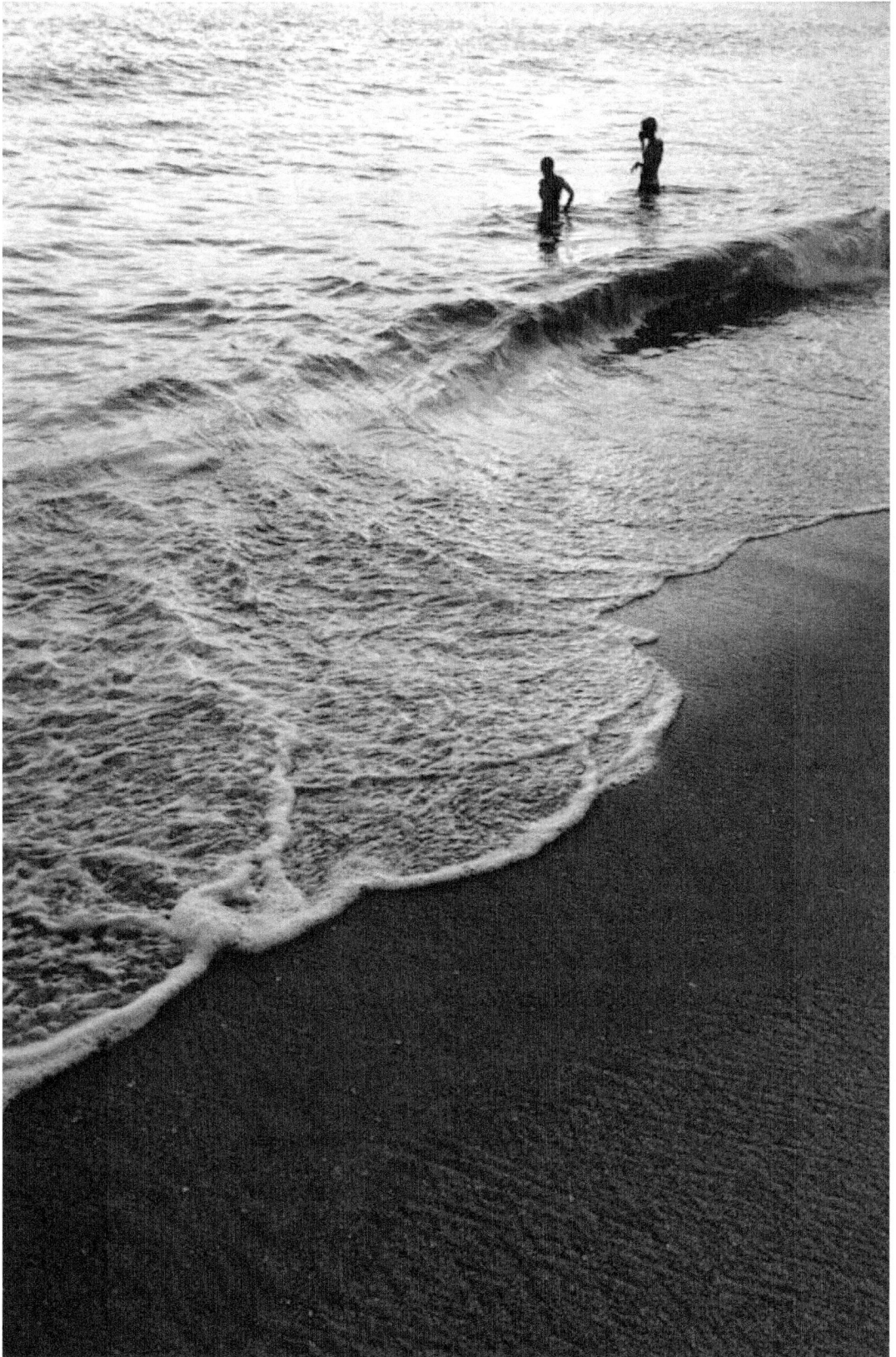

Seed Of Light

I've done it again,

Grown accustomed to the darkness,

As if I were the sky

that never birthed a single star,

A moonless, dark night.

Once more, I've left my spirit

amidst the growing gloom,

As if the earth were sterile,

Devoid of a single nourishing seed,

A lost soul among all that grays.

How I wish to hang from the sky

Like a nourishing seed.

To be incandescent,

Fluorescent, soul to sky,

Opening ribcage to earth,

Sharing my warmth

So the soil can bloom again.

Bleak Sky

The clouds are bleak and blue,

They seem to want to stay a while,

Adhering to the sky as if they were glued.

The sky is veiled in gloom,

It must be getting close to day's end

Because it all seems ghostly up high.

This air feels heavy, so heavy to breathe,

Taking in all this dread,

As if we were all barely living at all.

Perhaps we must swallow this day whole

And start anew again tomorrow.

Blink A Wish

As I close my lids, our universe slips away,

In one blink, its secrets unveil.

I once imagined you'd return,

Hopeful, but time weathers me,

And your memory evaporates into stardust.

Perhaps I should fully welcome this void,

Allow it to fade into the ether,

Yet in the elemental stir,

Our love fades into silence.

So I close my lids one last time,

And wish you near, just one more time.

This time, I won't blink; I'll keep them shut,

Praying your face won't dissolve into the stars.

Bleached Scene

Voices smolder with fear,

Words bleached to keep pure,

It all seems like a perfect scene,

Yet they're all blindfolded against their will,

Remaining pegs in a chess game.

It's easier this way, they say,

Dragging silence through the bones.

Sins In Green

There is so much green here, eternal life,

The earth is always in bloom,

always noisy with bees and birds.

I'm touched by this beauty,

I take it all in as if it were my own breath,

I feel as if I am no one in this space.

This place is too pure for someone who sins,

I've shed my skin and clothes to feel pure,

I've given my body to the earth to be healed,

But my eyes will not shut to the past I've lived,

My skin is like leather to this soul,

I'm left bare with bones.

Always Raising

4

And I decided long ago

that letting go was the same

as blooming.

Unveiling Me

This year, I'll just be me,

wild, funny, and unapologetically free.

Like the sun, I'll rise,

and as the moon, I'll set,

embracing each moment,

without room for regret.

I will be a night creature,

exploring the darkness,

counting infinite stars,

and will laugh with fireflies

that weave through leaves.

This year, it's all about me,

effortless self-love,

and humbly letting go.

Shhhh...

listen in the stillness,

it is there that magic happens.

Wild Learning

I'm still learning my wild,

In this ever-changing season's flow,

I'm an earth child within nature's mold.

Sometimes, I feel as if I were

this magic, bold,

Like a celestial sun.

My light healing, warm and old.

But in truth,

I'm just a woman,

Untamed, yet gentle,

Ready to love with my entirety.

A New Journey

In the cycle of loss,

a new phoenix emerged,

from the ashes of failure,

wisdom was born,

an indomitable spirit, undeterred.

I embraced the journey,

tattered and torn.

in shattered fragments,

I found strength.

That Power

Some shine so brightly

that they can bring entire

forests to ashes with their flame.

I like to see how it burns—

there's something about that power

that fills me with strength.

Unclouded Nature

I'm colorless, transparent by nature,

Pure and unclouded by affection or aversion.

I'm genuine, honest to the marrow.

You'll find me in some natural passage,

Contemplating its beauty, seated and writing.

What sets me apart from most is my soul,

my giving nature. It's innate to me.

Some envy my transparency,

Wishing I were black or white, opaque.

Yet I possess a single entity, unlike them,

Ready to be shared with a joyful heart.

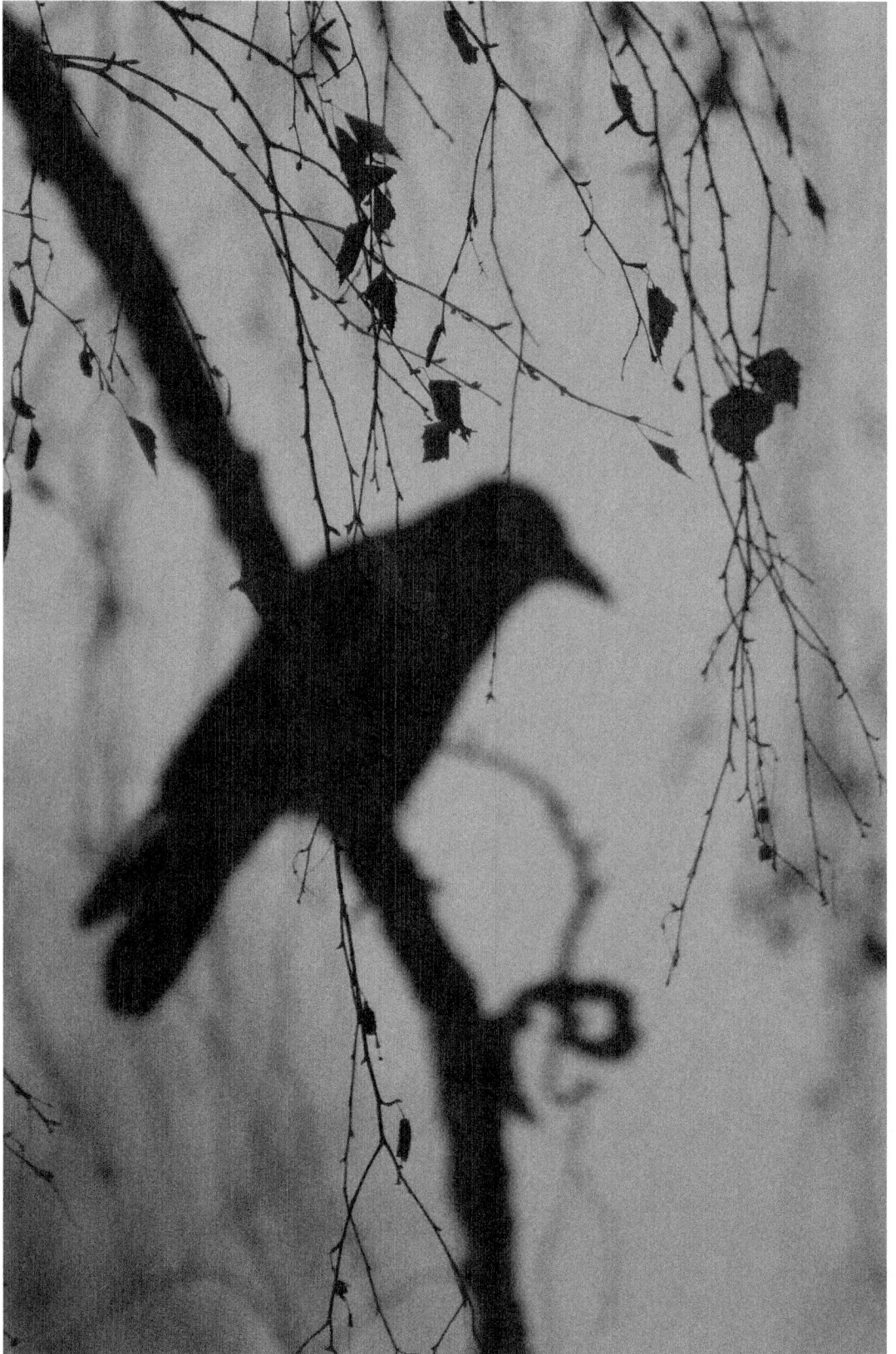

Solid Ground

The soil I stood on

Felt dry and firm,

A relief in knowing

I wouldn't fall

As I did that day.

No ice, no slipping,

This ground felt stable

—my life, at ease.

After my accident,

There was nothing left to lose,

And when you've lost it all,

When life has shown its horrors,

It's in moments like these,

You learn to live again.

I am a fierce creature,

Needing to protect all that I love.

Cultivating a wild softness,

Learning to release,

What no longer serves me.

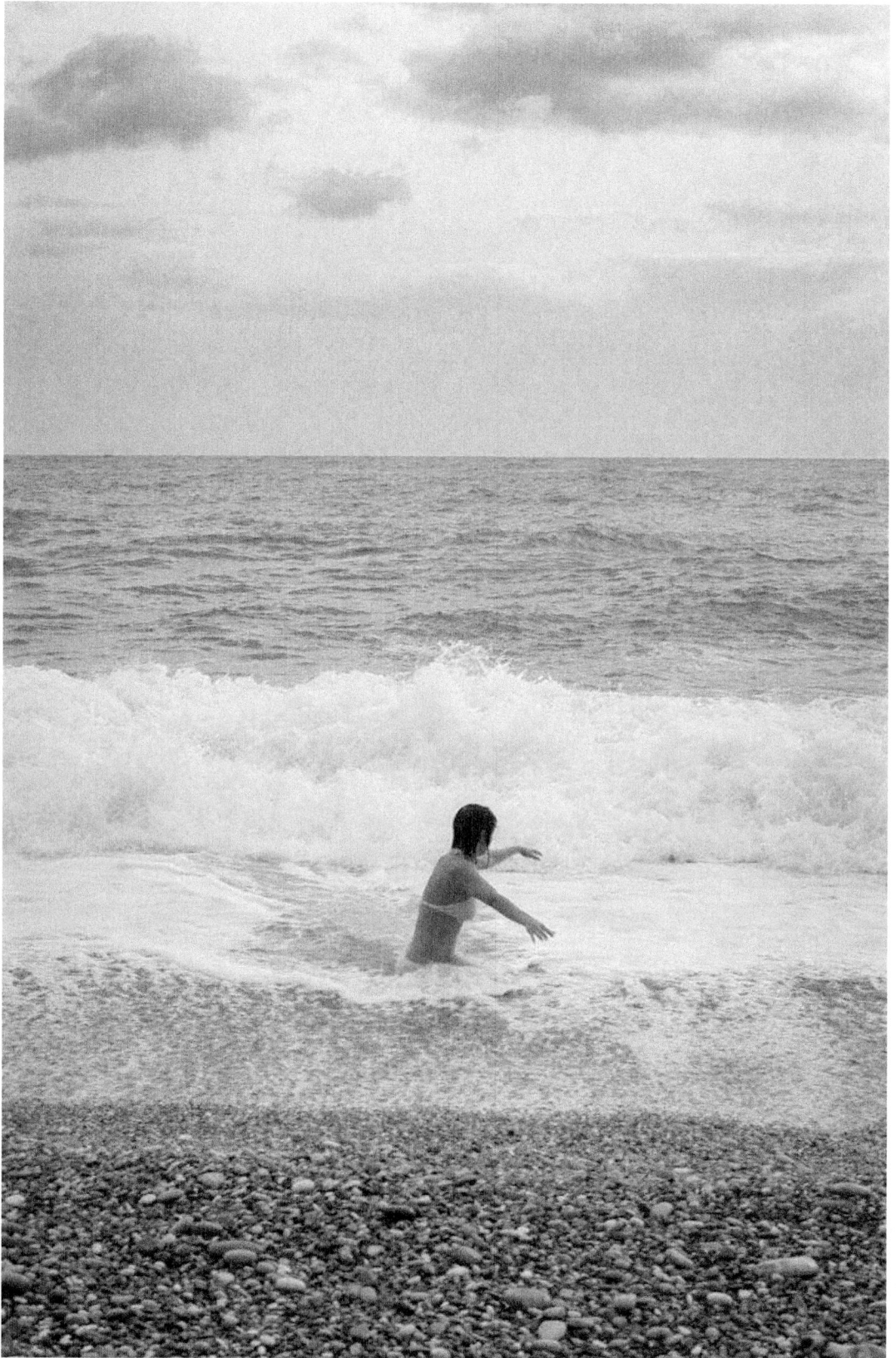

Sunny Days

I'm the summer's warmth,

My sunny presence fills the air

Fields sway with golden wheat,

Crickets chirp around me.

I'm all golden and warm,

Like the vibrant colors of a summer sunset.

Fields stretch with endless green,

The sun's warmth blankets all.

And the moving crops,

Reflect my sense of untamed spirit.

Marred Marrow

Stand properly jointed and tall,

Gluing all fragments left in the bones.

Remember the slow mourning

That brought you back to life.

It's time to refrain from those

Who poison the marrow.

Wear your smile proudly

And feel it to your skullcap.

It's time to free yourself

from what is tainted.

The waves,

silent poets of the sea,

echo their words

beneath the ocean's surface

Watercolor

Beneath the canopy

Of azure skies,

The violets and dahlias

Are welcomed once more

As the morning sun

Kisses the earth.

A vivid kaleidoscope of hues

Greets me upon awakening.

In the garden where dreams bloom,

It breathes of soft florals

And feels like spring.

The verdant land lies still,

While bees dance with butterflies.

I'm in love with its pulsating life,

I want to accept its ample offering,

And become a watercolor

That dissolves into its endless beauty.

Rebirth

I feel this widening in my heart,

pulling of my ribcage,

like birds falling from above,

my heart beating against its walls.

It's time, it's time, it's time.

I will shed the skin that dresses me

until my soul's nudeness births again,

pure, uncomplicated, and happy.

It's time, it's time, it's time.

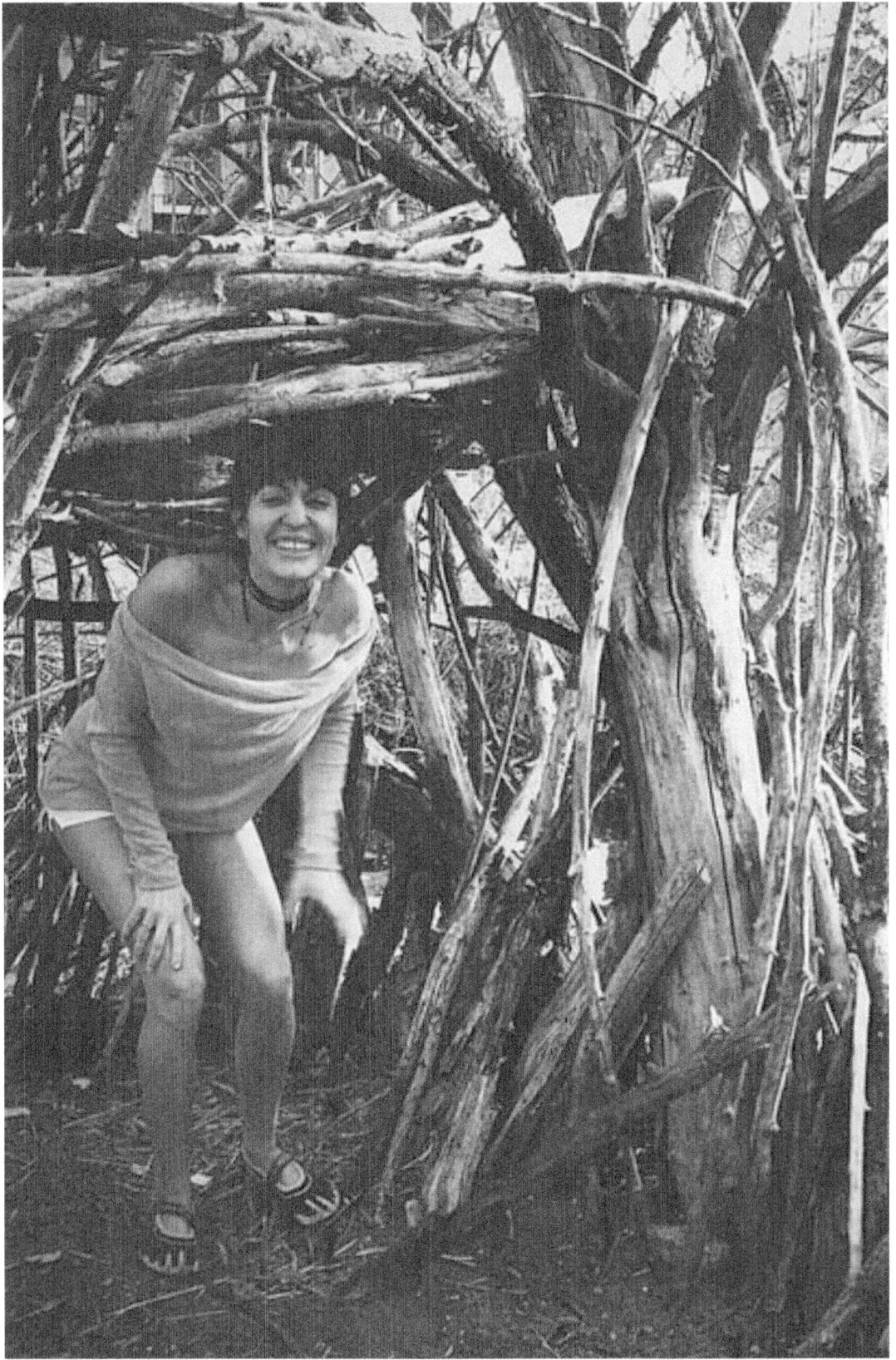

Most days, I am less of you,

and more of me, and continue

to need more of myself to be human.

Golden Eye

In the sky's divine heaven,

The gold eye of God wakes,

Gazing over Mother Earth.

Morning breaks with its light,

Sunlight pours as liquid gold,

A sacred kiss, pure and tender.

The glowing ember rises high,

It breathes life,

Painting souls in yellow.

When the day softly dims,

And the sky mellows down,

The holy eye closes gently,

Leaving stars to wash over darkness.

Night's Messenger

The raven visits me,

Stark black majesty,

A night's cunning creature,

Harbinger of hope's omen.

Each end a genesis, it reminds me,

Its feathered beauty, under-appreciated,

Your wings, a silken night shroud, ascend.

Allow me to fly upon

your soft black feathered back,

Show me the omens of my ancestors.

Earthly Soil

Upon the hillside,

I sense life underfoot.

Soil—my mother, cool,

cradles life and death.

Heavy and cold,

yet soft and nurturing.

On alien land,

my spirit surrenders.

Voices of the earth

speak in my native tongue.

A pleasant voice—this moment,

one with the soil, breath its voice.

Soul Of The Wildwood

The wildwood forest

Breathes deep within me,

Untamed and fearless,

I wander, wild and free.

Its beauty and wilderness

Carve a sanctuary where I find truths

In nourishing depths,

Where I am whole again.

I'm the wildwood that blooms,

The wind that kisses the trees,

A nomad of earth and soil,

A seed of hope awaiting to sprout,

Becoming a sacred woman,

I roam, unblamed and pure.

Perfectly Imperfect

The most beautiful things in life

Are those which are imperfect by nature.

I find them pure, vulnerably inviting,

Unique, rare, and captivating.

In a world where the outer shell

Of looking perfect is favored,

I go against the grain, I'm a rebel,

And that in itself is truly beautiful.

Cooler In Purity

I let my sins shed like skin,

Feels like carrying a paperweight.

They're like rabbits,

Seven litters before meeting their fate.

Once shed, I'm bare, from toe to head,

Cooler in my purity.

Time to make my bed,

Lay to rest.

By The Shore

I face the ocean,

black sand, mossy pebbles entwined,

salt traces purity,

healing with its touch.

Soft sun strokes the waves,

ocean's warm embrace,

a living painting,

blues deepen in water.

I'm just a woman,

by the shore standing firm,

color palette washing my feet,

cleansing me anew.

Seed To Soul

I am rooted deeply,

Seeping life from the earth.

The rain softens the soil,

A malleable living thing

that wants to nourish.

In this fertile ground,

I allow myself to grow,

Like a seed that becomes

a woman with soul.

All That Is Lost

In the delicate art of losing,

a nuanced art unfolds,

possessions slipping away,

a script the universe holds.

As if these belongings seek escape,

in a fate they reshape.

Amidst this chaos,

I lose fragments of myself.

The city, once a sanctuary,

now lost in the past.

I feel this feeling will last.

In the acceptance of what's gone,

I miss it all,

a song of losses,

an inevitable call.

Yet, I've found that

in the acceptance

of each loss,

I discover resilience,

a pathway to survive the cross.

After all, this too shall pass,

a mantra to hold,

a story to unfold.

Blossoming Woman

I'm growing into a soft-spoken woman,

And shedding the old engraved belief

That I'm not enough.

Perhaps it's time to enjoy slow mornings

And watch the season as it births spring.

Appreciate the small moments that come and go

And hold onto the hope that is left in people.

After all, in those moments—it is that I may bloom.

We are the cosmos encased in skin,

awaiting to burst into stars

while leaving trails of stardust

behind, as proof we hold

the Universe inside.

Unveiling Miracles

My magic's cradled deep

within my heart's right ventricle,

ready to burst forth

at the sight of kindness.

I've learned to harness it,

so I can unveil to all

that miracles do exist.

Earthly Miracles

They say the eyes reflect the cosmos,

For we are stardust, born of celestial grace.

Like astral angels, we stand on soil,

Our plumes shed to journey this earthly space.

I lift my lids, peering into my pupils,

Admiring a brown-golden galaxy's hue.

Lashes fluttering like forgotten wings,

A reminder of the soil I'm rooted to.

Golden stars cling like barbs to the sky,

I'm reminded of my flesh and frame,

Human, yet divine in Gaia's eye.

Within my stare, I see the vastness of the ocean,

the earth's enduring strength.

I'm one with this sacred Earth

A miracle to witness since my first breath.

Transformed

Despite all I've faced,

When most expected me to stumble,

Past the tears I've cried and anger I've felt,

In the face of life's unfair horrors,

Leaving dreams forgotten and untouched,

I'll rise, light as air,

I'll climb to the heavens, starting over,

I'll choose my fate, I'll live under a new sun,

Create fresh dreams to share,

Even with scars that persist,

I'll emerge changed by it all.

Lazy Sundays

Sundays have turned into

warm, lazy lounging days,

where I bask beneath the bright sun,

lost in beloved poetry,

and sipping cool herbal tea.

I relish the unhurried pace,

finding joy in baking cherished recipes

while tending to my lilies,

jasmine, and garden strawberries.

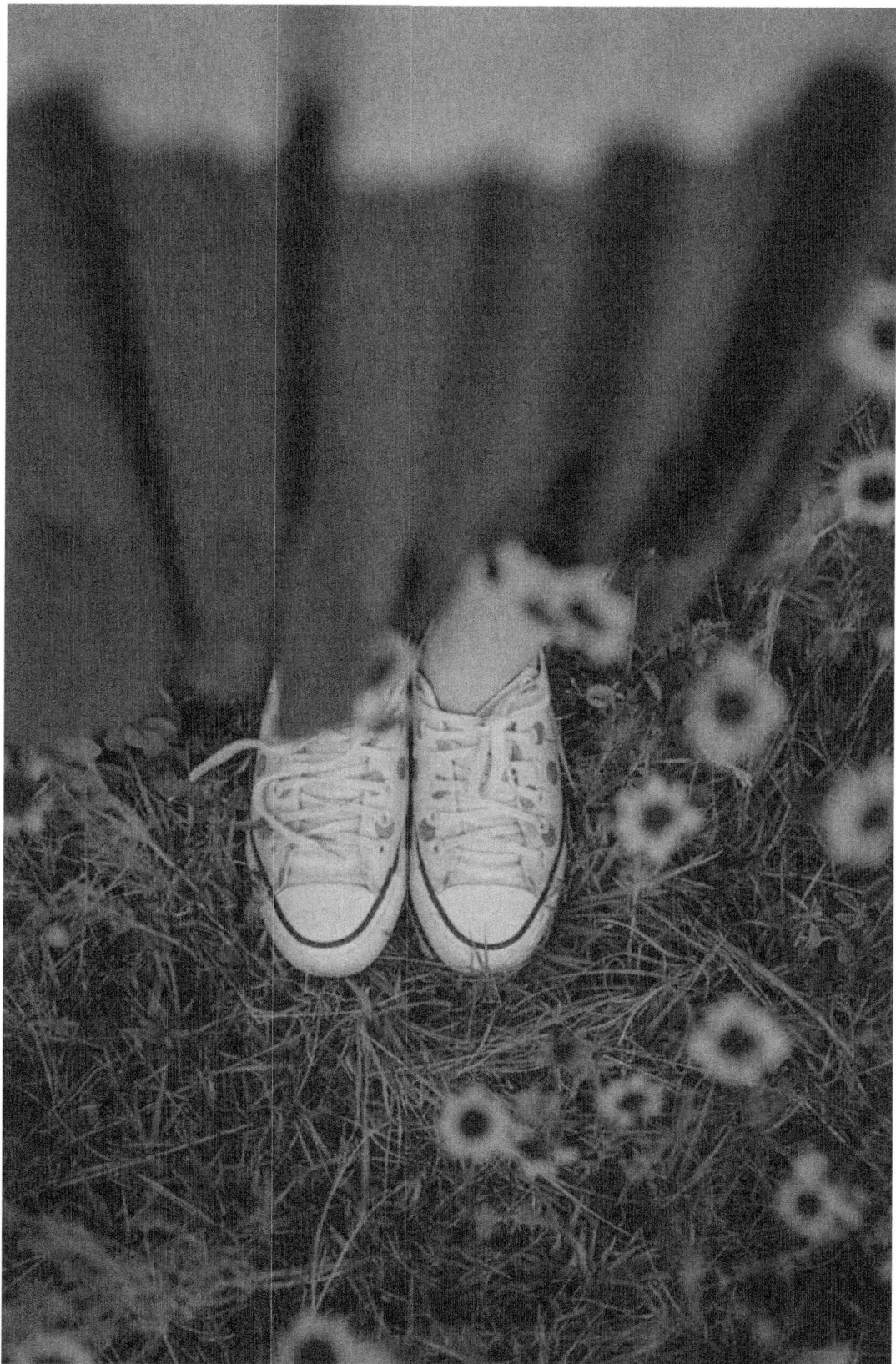

Newborn

I'm excited for spring's arrival,

Where tender buds swell with life's survival,

And rain soaks the waiting soil.

Grass sprouts, putting forth its roots,

While trees welcome their leafy recruits—

A magnificent scene to behold.

Spring, the season of aliveness,

It stirs my heart, with joy so boundless,

Pulsating with life's force,

Greeting my body, alive.

Spring reminds me, ever so,

How life is born to die, a truth we know.

The sun rises, its touch a scorch,

Yet all blooms in nature's torch.

In a bird's song, nature's call,

Let it all be born again, wild and free,

Like a newborn child, freshly born.

When fear wraps tightly

around your skin,

shed it as you would old skin.

It's very liberating.

About The Author

Born in the Canary Islands, Spain, Virginia Guarddon's roots run deep. While she spent most of her life in the USA, her heart always held the echoes of her island home.

From the age of 6, words became Virginia's refuge—a way to release emotions onto paper. After majoring in Science and minoring in Piano Performance at the University of Central Oklahoma, life led her to blend holistic skincare and poetry in Breckenridge, CO.

Her dreams took a hit with a brutal accident, temporarily robbing her ability to walk and leaving behind a trail of loss—business, home, everything. Amidst this upheaval, Virginia also endured the challenge of being separated from her husband. Seeking solace, she returned to the Canary Islands, striving to make it possible for him to join her in Spain. In the midst of these challenges, she faced the arduous task of rebuilding her life.

Chapter 1:

Nature is My Healer Nature, a profound healer,
cradled Virginia in its embrace. Supported by the
softness of wind and the earth's strength, this
section reveals the delicate interplay between
nature and the human spirit. The rhythmic waves of
the ocean whispered serenity, calming not only her
troubled mind but also resonating through her
family.

Chapter 2:

My Muse, Our Love In Virginia's life, love takes
center stage. "My Muse, Our Love" delves into the
heartache and resilience of a love tested by
distance. Threads stretched thin, the poems explore
the tender moments, the ache of missing, and the
strength found in shared dreams. It's a subtle
interplay of two souls connected across miles,
finding solace in the shared warmth of memories and
the anticipation of a shared future.

Chapter 3:

Life is Hard "Life is Hard" confronts brutal truths.
In this section, she allows the rawness of sadness
to flow, a crucial step in the journey to heal. Each
poem is a raw stroke on the canvas of her soul,
depicting the agony of loss, the echoes of despair,
and the slow emergence of resilience. It's an
exploration of the darkest corners of the human
experience, a brave confrontation with pain, and a
testament to the strength found in vulnerability.

Chapter 4:

Always Rising "Always Rising" chronicles Virginia's
emergence into the light. This section is an ode to
her indomitable spirit, celebrating her upward
journey and the forging of a path to a renewed self.
Here, she delves into the complexities of rebuilding
—a composition of strength, determination, and the
resilience to rise from the ashes. Each poem is a
step forward, a testament to her enduring spirit,
and an exploration of the power of rising, again
and again.

Free The Bird" is a journey of rebirth, a poetic
narrative of finding oneself amidst the ruins and
soaring anew.

Author Virginia Guarddon (Wildwood Writer)

Free the bird within you,

It's time, it's time...

Printed in Great Britain
by Amazon